How Artists Use

Perspective

Paul Flux

Heinemann Library
Chicago, Illinois

Designed by Celia Floyd
Illustrations by Jo Brooker/Ann Miller
Originated by Ambassador Litho Ltd.
Printed and bound in Hong Kong/China

05 04 03 02 01
10 9 8 7 6 5 4 3 2

Library of Congress Cataloging-in-Publication Data
Flux, Paul, 1952-
       Perspective / Paul Flux.
          p. cm.
       Includes bibliographical references (p.) and index.
       ISBN 1-58810-080-4 (lib. bdg.)
       1. Perspective--Juvenile literature. 2. Drawing--Technique--Juvenile literature. 3.
   Painting--Technique--Juvenile literature. [1. Perspective. 2. Drawing--Technique. 3.
Painting--Technique.] I. Title.

NC750 .F59 2001
750'.1'8--dc21
                                                    00-058150

Acknowledgments
The Publishers would like to thank the following for permission to reproduce photographs:
© ADAGP, Paris and DACS, London 2001, p. 26; AKG, London/Art Institute of Chicago, pp. 6, 7; Bern, Klee Foundation/© DACS 2001, p. 21; National Gallery, London, pp.18, 19; Tate Gallery, London, p. 17; Art Archive/© ADAGP, Paris and DACS, London, 2001, p. 16; Bridgeman Art Library/National Gallery, London, pp. 4, 14, Bridgeman Art Library/© ADAGP, Paris and DACS, London, 2001, p. 20; *Ascending and Descending* by M. C. Escher, ©2000 Cordon Art B.V.-Baarn-Holland. All rights reserved, p. 11; National Gallery of Scotland, Edinburgh, p. 12; National Trust Photographic Library/Derrick E. Witty, p. 13; San Francisco Art Institute/David Wakely, p. 9; SCALA/Collection Gianni Mattioli, Milan/© DACS 2001, p. 15; Städtisches Museum Abteiberg, Möchengladbach/© The Andy Warhol Foundation for the Visual Arts, Inc./DACS, London, 2001. Trademarks licensed by Campbell Soup Company. All Rights Reserved, p. 29; 2001 The Museum of Modern Art, New York, p. 28, /© DACS, London VAGA, New York, 2001, p. 24; Yale University Art Gallery, New Haven, Connecticut/© DACS 2001, p. 22.

Cover photograph reproduced with permission of Bridgeman Art Library.

Every effort has been made to contact copyright holders of any material reproduced in this book.
Any omissions will be rectified in subsequent printings if notice is given to the Publisher.

Some words are in bold, **like this.** You can find
out what they mean by looking in the glossary.

Contents

What Is Perspective?

Perspective is a way that artists can make a painting seem to have distance and **depth.** This painting was done on a flat **surface,** but perspective makes the picture look almost real.

Carlo Crivelli,
***The Annunciation with Saint Emidius,* 1486**

This is how perspective works. These three **figures** are all the same size. But their position on the page and the lines in the drawing make them look as though they are different sizes.

Lines of Perspective

Gustave Caillebotte, *Paris Street, Rainy Day,* 1877

When you look at a painting that has been done in **perspective,** it might seem as though you are looking through a window. Artists make the things that are supposed to be far away very small and close to each other.

6

In this painting, the lines on the street and the buildings all seem to come together in one spot on the **horizon.** The place where the lines meet is called the **vanishing point.**

Fooling Your Eyes

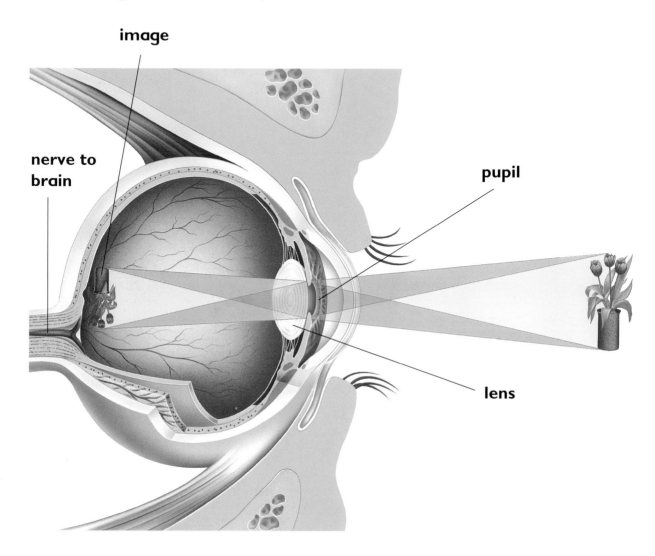

image

nerve to brain

pupil

lens

When you look at something, you are really seeing the light that an object gives off. Your eyes change the light into electrical signals that go to your brain. Your brain turns the signals into an **image.** This all happens very fast.

Diego Rivera, *The Making of a Fresco Showing the Building of a City*, 1931

Each of your eyes sees things at a slightly different angle. Your brain puts these two images together, so that you see things as having **three dimensions.**

Optical Illusions

Perspective is an **optical illusion**—a trick of the eye. At first glance, you might think that what is shown in a drawing or painting is real. This is because your brain is used to seeing things in **three dimensions.**

When you first look at this picture, you might think that it is just a drawing of people on the roof of a building. But when you look carefully, you see that the people are going around in a loop. The artist has used perspective to fool your eyes!

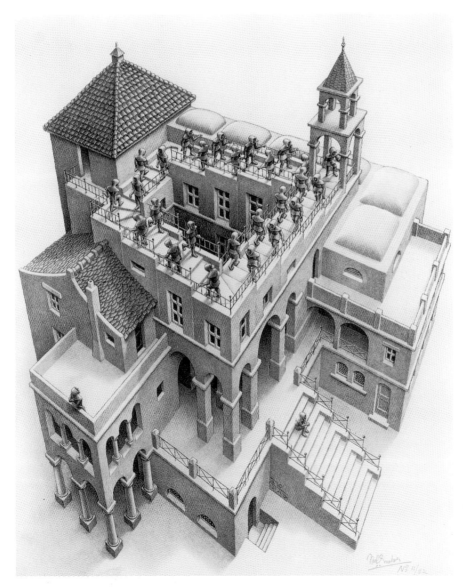

M. C. Escher,
Ascending and
Descending, 1960

Perspective Inside

Artists can use **perspective** to show how large something is. This artist has painted a group of very small people in the lower left-hand corner of this painting. It adds to the **optical illusion** that the building is very large and tall.

Pieter Saenredam,
Interior of St. Bavo's
Church, 1648

Samuel van Hoogstraten, *A View down a Corridor*, 1662

Perspective can also give you the feeling that you are looking down a long hall. Look very carefully at the picture. The doors and the table are real, but the hallway is a painting! Paintings like this are called ***trompe-l'oeil.***

Antonio Canaletto, *The Basin of San Marco on Ascension Day*, about 1740

This is a painting of Venice, a famous city in Italy. The artist wanted to show his home city on the day of an important festival. He used lines of **perspective** to make the city look very large.

Giorgio de Chirico,
Disquieting Muses, 1916

Perspective usually makes pictures look real, but this artist used perspective to create a feeling of things being all mixed up. The objects are casting strange shadows. The **figure** in the middle of the painting has a tiny head, and the box in the **foreground** gets wider at the back instead of getting narrower.

Perspective, Light, and Color

Artists also show **perspective** with light and color.
Things that appear close up have sharp outlines.
Things that seem far away look fuzzy. At the **horizon**,
the sky appears lighter than the sky overhead!

Claude Monet, *La Gare St.-Lazare*, 1877

This artist painted steam from the trains and mist to create a sense of space and distance in this painting. Although you can't really see the **vanishing point,** the lines of the train tracks seem to lead far into the distance.

William Turner, *Rain, Steam, and Speed,* about 1844

Paolo Uccello, *The Battle of San Romano,* 1450–1460

Perspective became very popular during the **Renaissance**. At first, artists had to **experiment** with the way perspective worked. In this painting, there are lots of **vanishing points,** so the picture is not very **realistic**.

Jan van Eyck,
The Arnolfini Portrait,
1434

This artist understood perspective so well that he could play little tricks with it. When you look at this painting, you feel as though you are looking through a window at a man and his wife. This feeling is even stronger because it seems that you can also see outside through the open window. Another trick is the reflection in the mirror—it shows another person in the room with the artist and the couple.

Playing with Perspective

By the early **twentieth century,** artists wanted to do something new. They tried **experiments** with **perspective**. This painter tried to show a **mandolin** from many different angles in the same painting. This **style** of painting is called **Cubism.**

Georges Braque,
The Mandolin,
1909–1910

Paul Klee,
Park near Lucerne,
1938

This artist decided to leave perspective out of this painting. He wanted to put everything on one **plane.** The painting is not **realistic.** Instead it shows the forms of everything you would see in a park.

Abstract Perspective

**El Lissitzky,
Proun 99,
about 1924**

This artist **experimented** with **perspective** using
abstract shapes and patterns. In this picture, a
wedge-shaped net seems as though it is coming out
of the picture toward you. You can make your own
painting using abstract shapes and perspective.

22

1. Draw a **vanishing point** on an imaginary **horizon**.
2. Draw three or four rectangles.
3. Use long, straight lines to connect three corners of each rectangle to the vanishing point.
4. Add some flat, abstract designs in between the rectangles. Color your design.

Perspective in Landscapes

Perspective can help create **landscapes.** There are not many things in this painting, but it is very **dramatic.** The white line makes the road look as though it runs far into the distance. You can paint your own dramatic landscape.

Allan D'Arcangelo, *US Highway 1, Number 5,* 1962

1. Cover a large piece of paper with a light blue **color wash**. Mix in a little white to change the **shade**.
2. When the paper dries, sketch a **horizon** line low across the paper. Put a **vanishing point** in the center of the line.
3. Draw large, medium, and small rectangles along the sides of the paper. The smallest rectangles should be near the vanishing point.
4. Add your own details, such as a road, trees, or people.

Perspective with Figures

Victor Vasarely, *Study of Perspective,* 1935

The lines of **perspective** in this painting lead your eyes straight back to the **vanishing point.** The **figures** almost seem to be floating out of the light at the back of the painting. Try your own perspective drawing that includes figures.

26

1. Draw a square or rectangle near the center of a piece of paper.
2. From each corner of the square, draw a line all the way out to the edge of the paper.
3. Add four or five more lines that come out from the sides of the square.
4. Color in some of the spaces. Make the colors closer to the square lighter to make it look as though light is coming from the middle of the picture.
5. Draw in some figures.

27

Thinking About Perspective

Edward Hopper, *Gas*, 1940

Artists have used **perspective** to show ordinary things in a new way. What are some of the things the artist has done to show space and distance in this painting?

1. The sky over the **horizon** is lighter than the sky overhead.
2. The lines of the bushes and the gas pumps lead your eyes to the "back" of the painting.
3. The writing on the gas station sign is blurry, as if it is far away.

Andy Warhol, *Campbell's Soup Can,* **1962**

Andy Warhol's art made people take a new look at some of the things they used every day. Which can looks as though it is farther away? What makes it seem that way?

1. The can on the right seems farther away than the can on the left.
2. Smaller objects appear to be farther away. The artist has also made the writing on the label a little blurrier on the smaller can.

Glossary

abstract kind of art that does not try to show people or things, but instead focuses on shape and color

color wash thin coating of watered-down paint made by wetting paper and then letting color flow onto it from a big brush

Cubism style of painting that uses simple shapes and shows each object from different angles in the same picture

depth feeling of space and distance in a picture

dramatic having a strong feeling or affect

experiment to repeat something in different ways until you like the result

figure shape that looks like a human but that does not look like a particular person

foreground part of a picture that looks closest

horizon imaginary place where the earth and the sky seem to meet

image copy of a person or object

landscape picture of outdoor scenery, such as fields, trees, and houses

mandolin musical instrument that looks like a small guitar

optical illusion image that appears different than it actually is

perspective way an artist draws or paints on a flat surface so that there seems to be space and distance in the picture

plane something that is flat or level

realistic way of painting that shows things exactly as we see them in real life

Renaissance time in Europe between 1400 and 1700 when there was much interest in art

shade darker or lighter version of a color

surface top part of something

style way that a picture is painted

three dimensions to seem to be tall, wide, and to take up space

trompe-l'oeil French words that mean "fools the eye"—kind of painting that looks as if it could be real (You say Trohmp-loy.)

twentieth century years 1900 through 1999

vanishing point imaginary spot in a picture at which all the lines in a painting seem to come together

More Books to Read

Cook, J. *Understanding Modern Art*. Tulsa, Okla.: EDC Publishing, 1999. An older reader can help you with this book.

Richardson, Joy. *Showing Distance in Art*. Milwaukee, Wisc.: Gareth Stevens, 1999.

Sturgis, Alexander. *Optical Illusions: Discover How Paintings Aren't Always What They Seem to Be*. New York: Sterling Publishers, 1996.

Index

Arts
music